MARIA MERIAN'S
BUTTERFLIES
COLOURING
BOOK

DRAWINGS FROM
THE ROYAL COLLECTION

ARCTURUS

The Royal Collection is among the largest and most
important art collections in the world, and one of
the last great European royal collections to remain
intact. A department of the Royal Household, Royal
Collection Trust is responsible for the care of the
Royal Collection and manages the public opening
of the official residences of the Queen. Income
generated from admissions and from associated
commercial activities contributes directly to the
Royal Collection Trust, a registered charity. Explore
the Royal Collection at www.royalcollection.org.uk.

ARCTURUS

This edition published in 2019 by Arcturus Publishing Limited
26/27 Bickels Yard, 151–153 Bermondsey Street,
London SE1 3HA.

Copyright © Arcturus Holdings Limited
All images Royal Collection Trust/© HM Queen Elizabeth II 2016
Black-and-white drawings by Duncan Smith

ISBN: 978-1-78428-637-8
CH005433NT
Supplier 29, Date 0119, Print run 8217

Printed in China

Created for children 10+

INTRODUCTION

From a young age, Maria Sibylla Merian (1647–1717) was fascinated by butterflies and moths, and their metamorphosis. As an adult she worked relentlessly to investigate the life cycles of insects in Europe and in South America, publishing her findings in a series of beautifully illustrated books.

In 1679 Merian issued her first publication on insect metamorphosis, *The Wonderful Transformation of Caterpillars and their Particular Plant Nourishment*. This book presented her studies of insects through written accounts and elegant engravings, showing each insect's life cycle on the plant on which it fed. Her *magnum opus*, however, was published 26 years later in 1705. Entitled *The Metamorphosis of the Insects of Suriname*, and dedicated to 'all lovers and investigators of nature', this was the product of two years of study in the Dutch South American colony, Suriname, and it is from this publication that many of the works illustrated here are taken.

Merian and her youngest daughter, Dorothea, travelled to Suriname in the summer of 1699. The dangerous and uncomfortable voyage lasted two months, taking them from Amsterdam to the Surinamese capital, Paramaribo. Here they joined a settlement of around 500 wooden houses, taking a house with a small garden, where they were able to raise specimens of plants collected from the local area. From here they also made many expeditions into the surrounding forest, as well as to outlying plantations, widening their search for examples of metamorphosis, making careful observations of the insects and plants they encountered and bringing specimens back to rear and study. Merian recorded their findings in minute detail, preparing to publish her discoveries on her return to Amsterdam.

In addition to the published volume of the *Metamorphosis*, Merian produced at least two luxury sets of illustrations from the book. One of these is now in the Royal Collection, having been acquired by George III in the second half of the eighteenth century for his large scientific library. Part printed and part hand-painted on vellum, these works were prized from the day of their production for their impressive combination of artistic skill and scientific rigour. Probably produced with the aid of her two daughters (who were equally talented artists), Merian's vibrant pictures convey the fascination with metamorphosis and with exotic flora and fauna that was her driving passion.

Merian was not the only seventeenth-century woman to engage in scientific experimentation, travel to South America or publish learned books, but she was one of the most extraordinary, leaving a formidable legacy across Europe in the fields of art and entomology. Her observations on Surinamese insects were quoted and discussed throughout the scientific world, while her approach to illustration was adopted by many who subsequently published on natural history and botany.

Supremely beautiful and rigorously truthful, Merian's works show us, as they did her first readers, the wonder of metamorphosis and the astounding beauty of the natural world.

KEY: LIST OF PLATES

1 Frangipani plant with Red Cracker Butterfly

2 Barbados Lily with Bullseye Moth and Leaf-Footed Bug

3 Citron with Monkey Slug Moth and Harlequin Beetle

4 Branch of Pomegranate with Lanternfly and Cicada

5 Cassava with White Peacock Butterfly and young Golden Tegu

6 Cotton bush with Helicopis Butterfly and Tiger Moth

7 Branch of Pomegranate and Menelaus Blue Morpho Butterfly

8 Branch of Banana with Bullseye Moth

9 Branch of *Duroia eriopila* with Zebra Swallowtail Butterfly

10 Branch of Pomelo with Green-Banded Urania Moth

11 Branch of Seville Orange with *Rothschildia* moth

12 Banana with Teucer Owl Butterfly and Rainbow Whiptail Lizard

13 Vanilla with Gulf Fritillary

14 Ripe Pineapple with Dido Longwing Butterfly

15 Castor Oil plant with Ricini Longwing Butterfly

16 Costus plant with Banana Stem Borer Moth

17 Cassava root with Garden Tree Boa, Sphinx Moth and Treehopper

18 Cotton-Leaf Physicnut with Giant Sphinx Moth

19 *Heliconia acuminata* with Southern Armyworm Moth

20 Branch of West Indian Cherry with Achilles Morpho Butterfly

21 Branch of the Gumbo-Limbo Tree with White Witch Moth

22 Provence Rose

23 Branch of Fig with Sphinx Moths

24 Confederate Rose with Androgeous Swallowtail Butterfly

25 Grape Vine with Gaudy Sphinx Moth

26 *Muellera frutescens* with Brush-Footed and Clearwing Butterflies

27 Prickly Custard Apple with Hawk Moth

28 Branch of Genipapo with Long-Horned Beetle

29 Branch of Nipple Fruit with Leaf Mantis and Bean Leafskeletonizer

30 Branch of Sour Guava with Melantho Tiger-wing Butterfly and Flannel Moth

31 Coffee Senna with Split-Banded Owlet Butterfly

32 Branch of an unidentified tree with Menelaus Blue Morpho Butterfly

33 Papaya plant with *Nymphidium* butterfly

34 Branch of Willow with Red Underwing and Puss Moths

35 Spanish Jasmine with Ello Sphinx Moth and Garden Tree Boa

36 Turk's Cap Lily

37 Yellow Mombin with unidentified butterfly

38 Milk Thistle

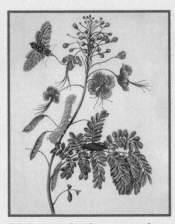

39 Peacock Flower with Carolina Sphinx Moth

40 Water Lemon with Snout Moth

41 Branch of Sour Guava with Carolina Sphinx Moth

42 Grape Vine with Vine Sphinx Moth and Satellite Sphinx Moth

43 Two Apples with Gypsy Moth

44 Branch of Cardinal's Guard with Idomeneus Giant Owl Butterfly

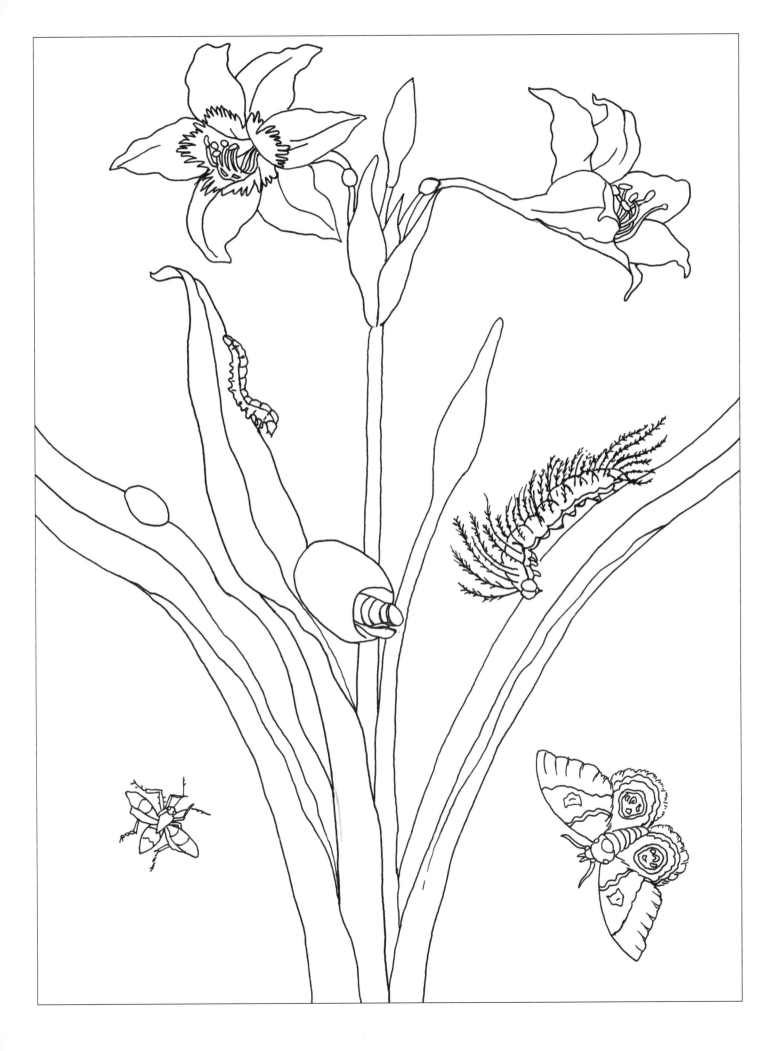

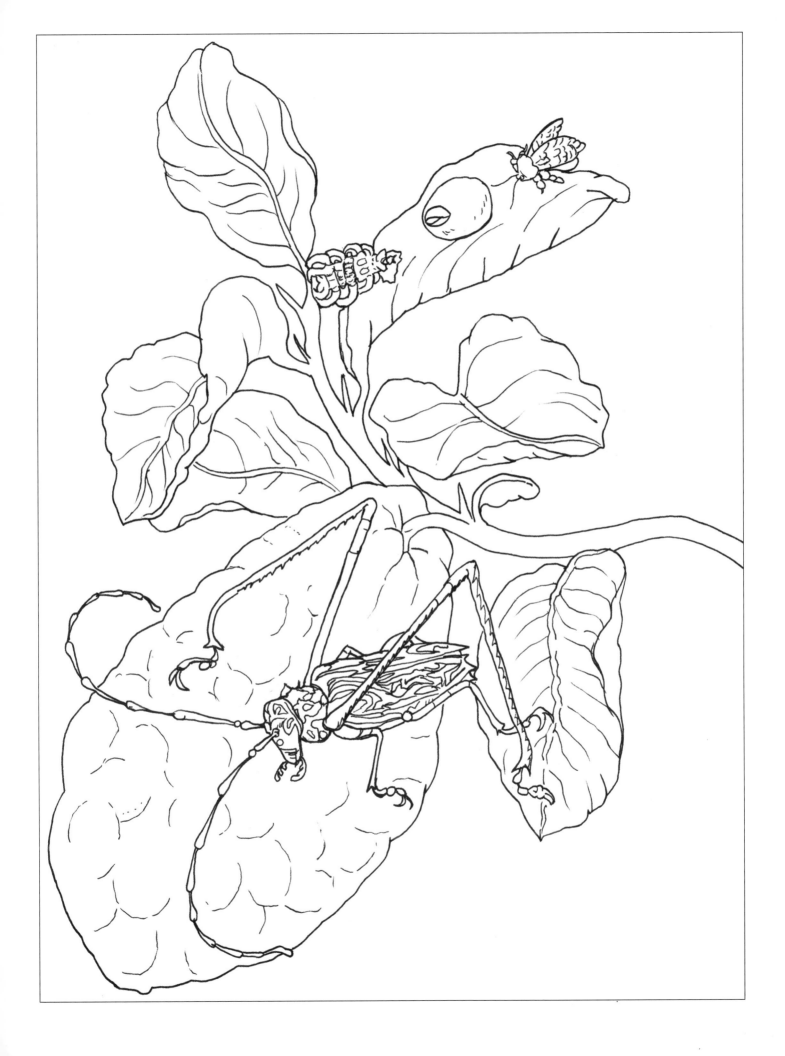

4

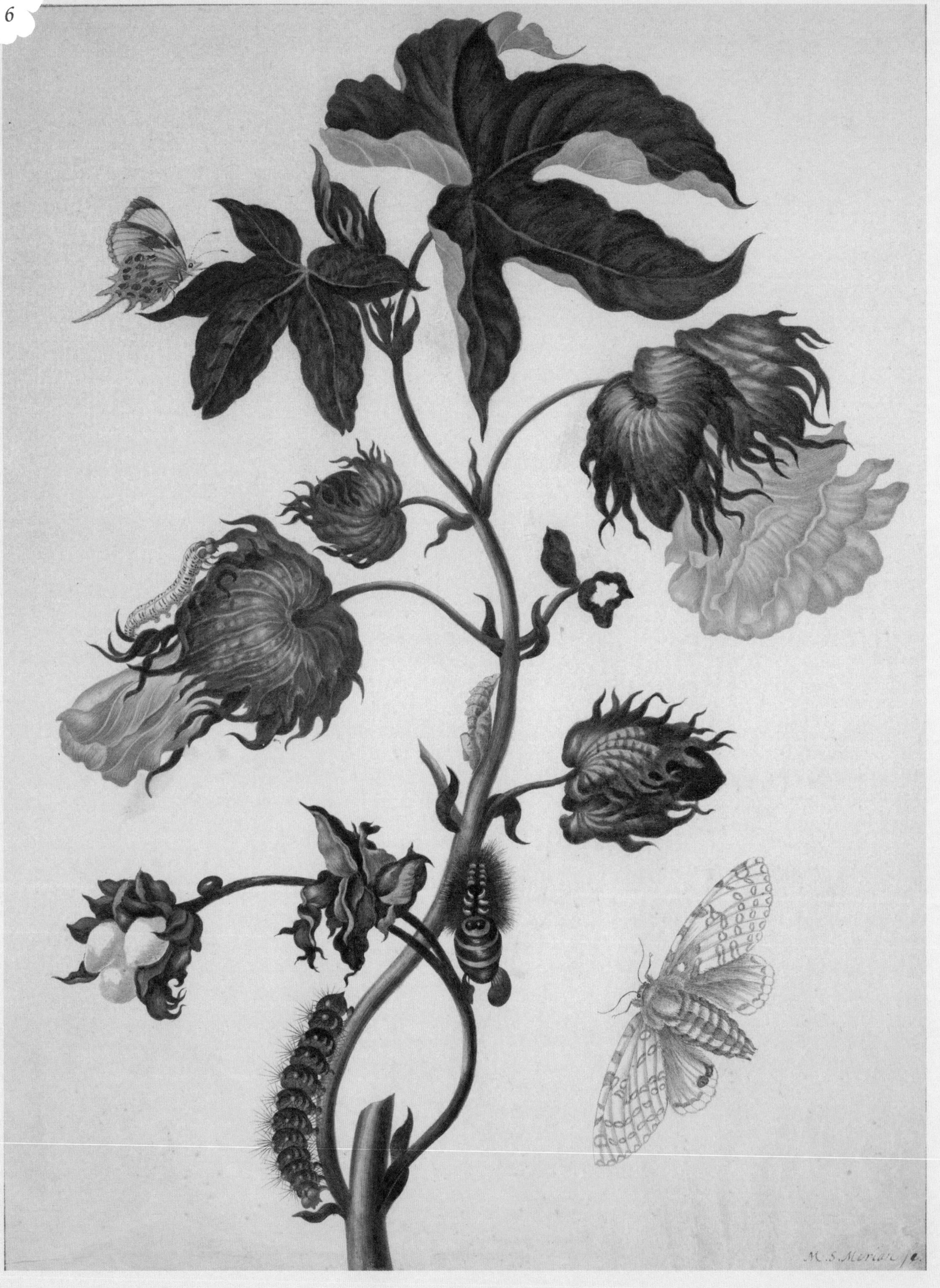
M. S. Merian fe.

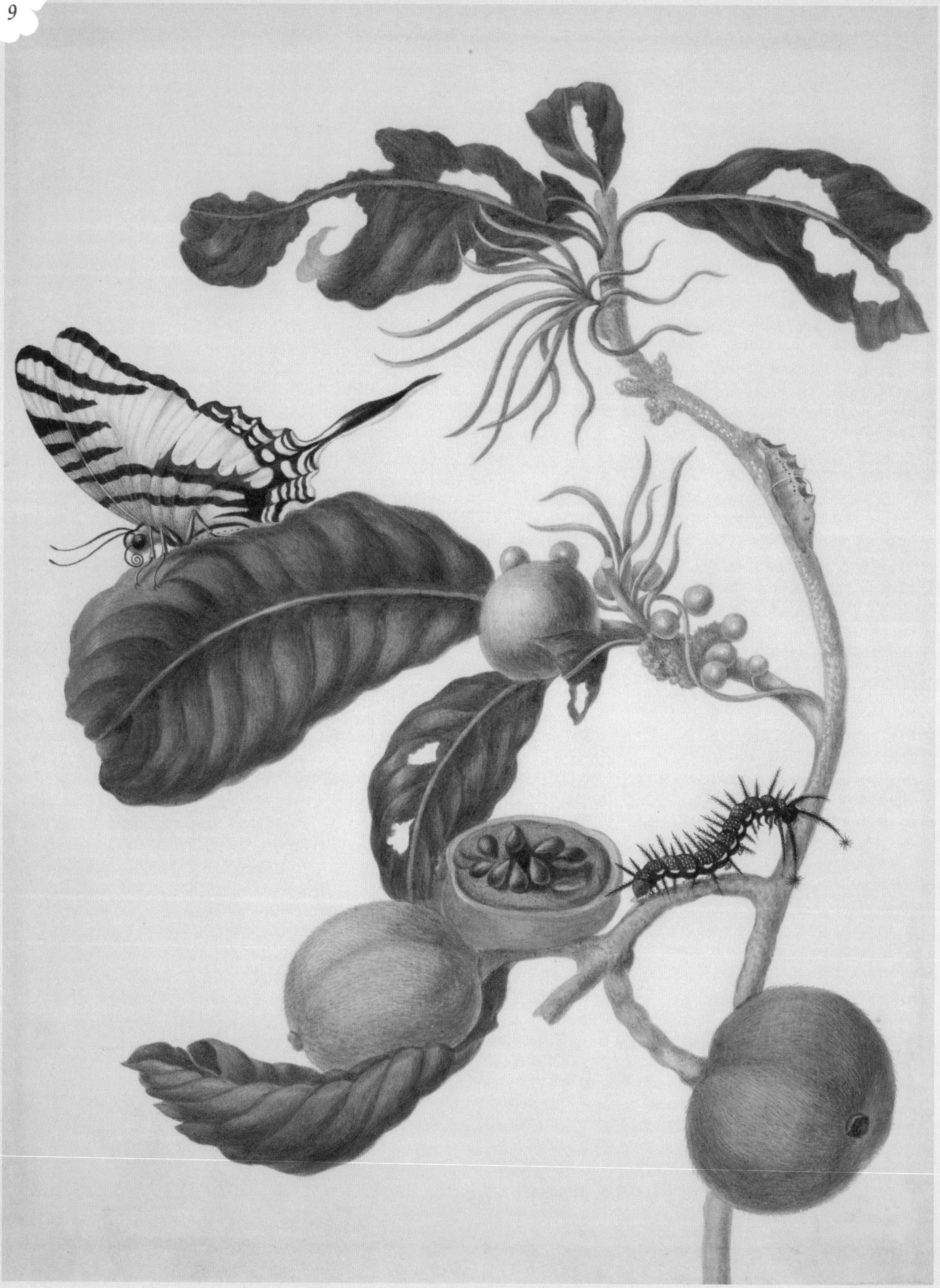

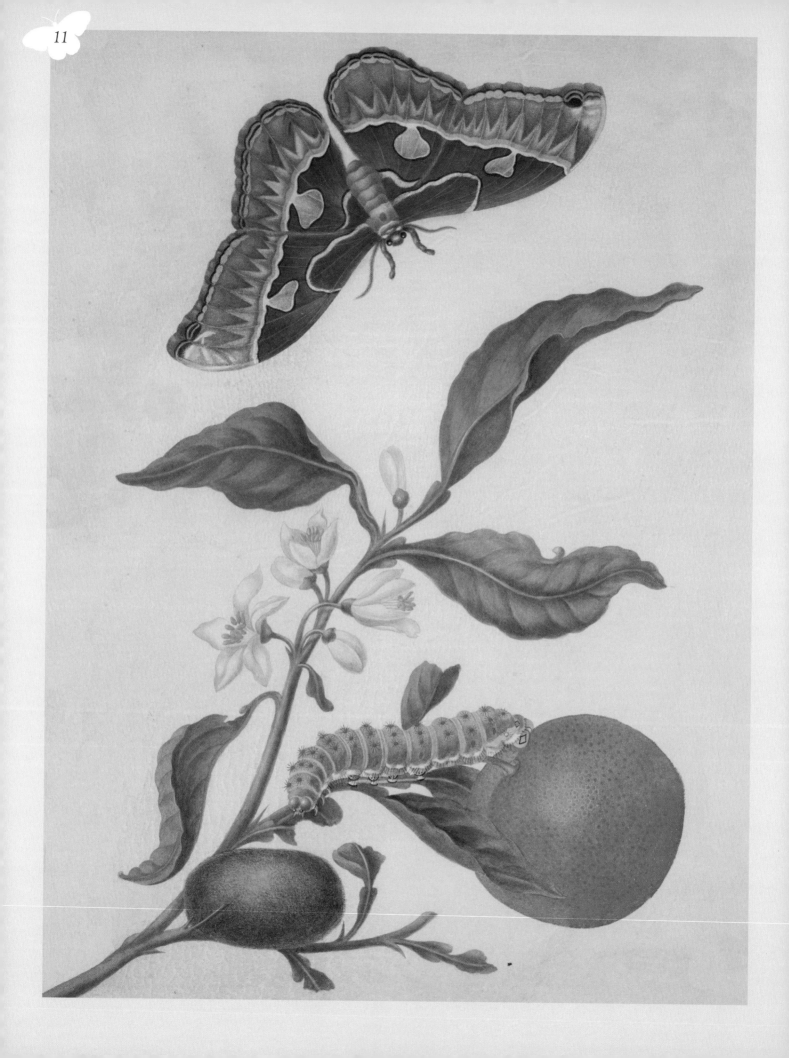

13

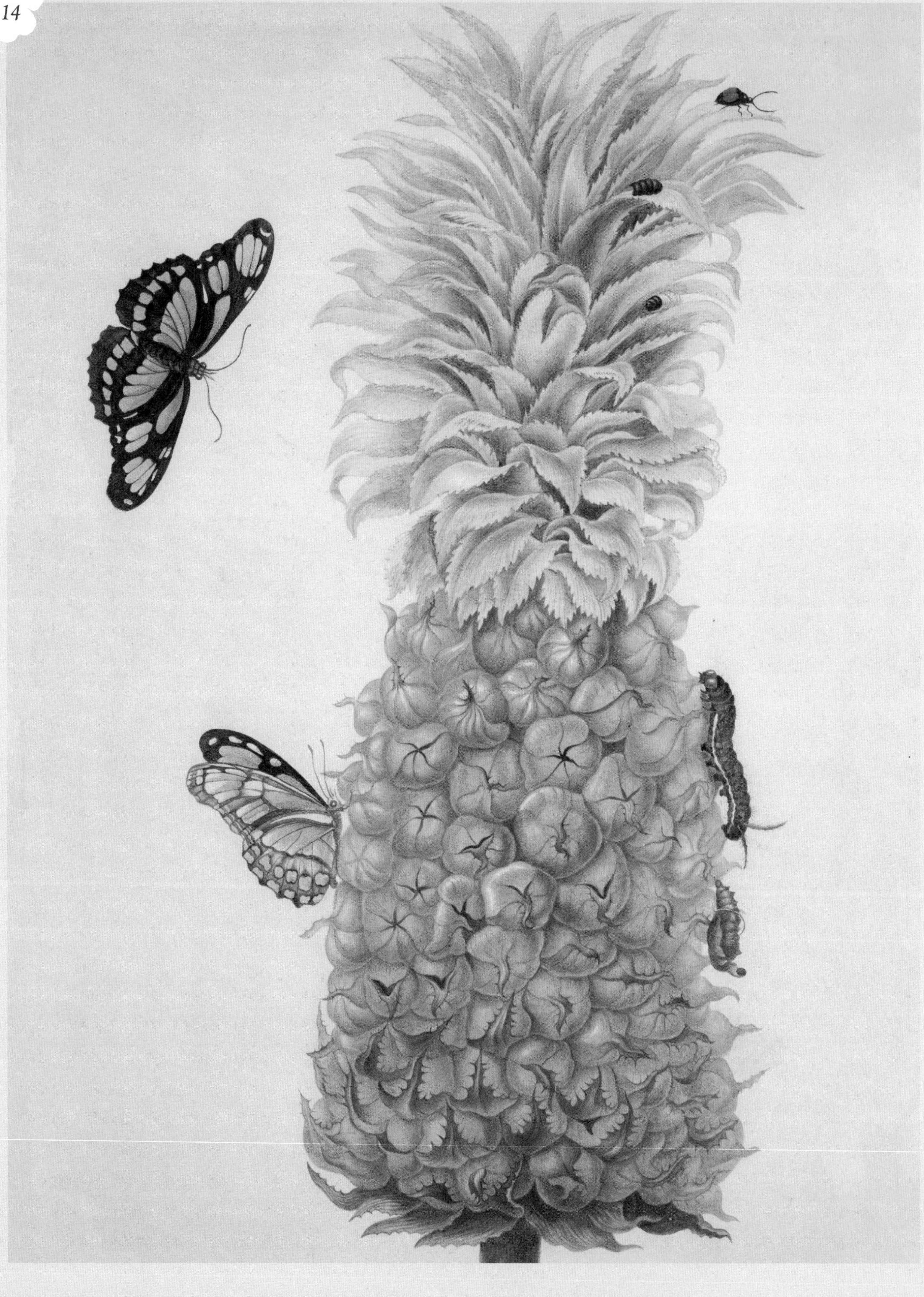

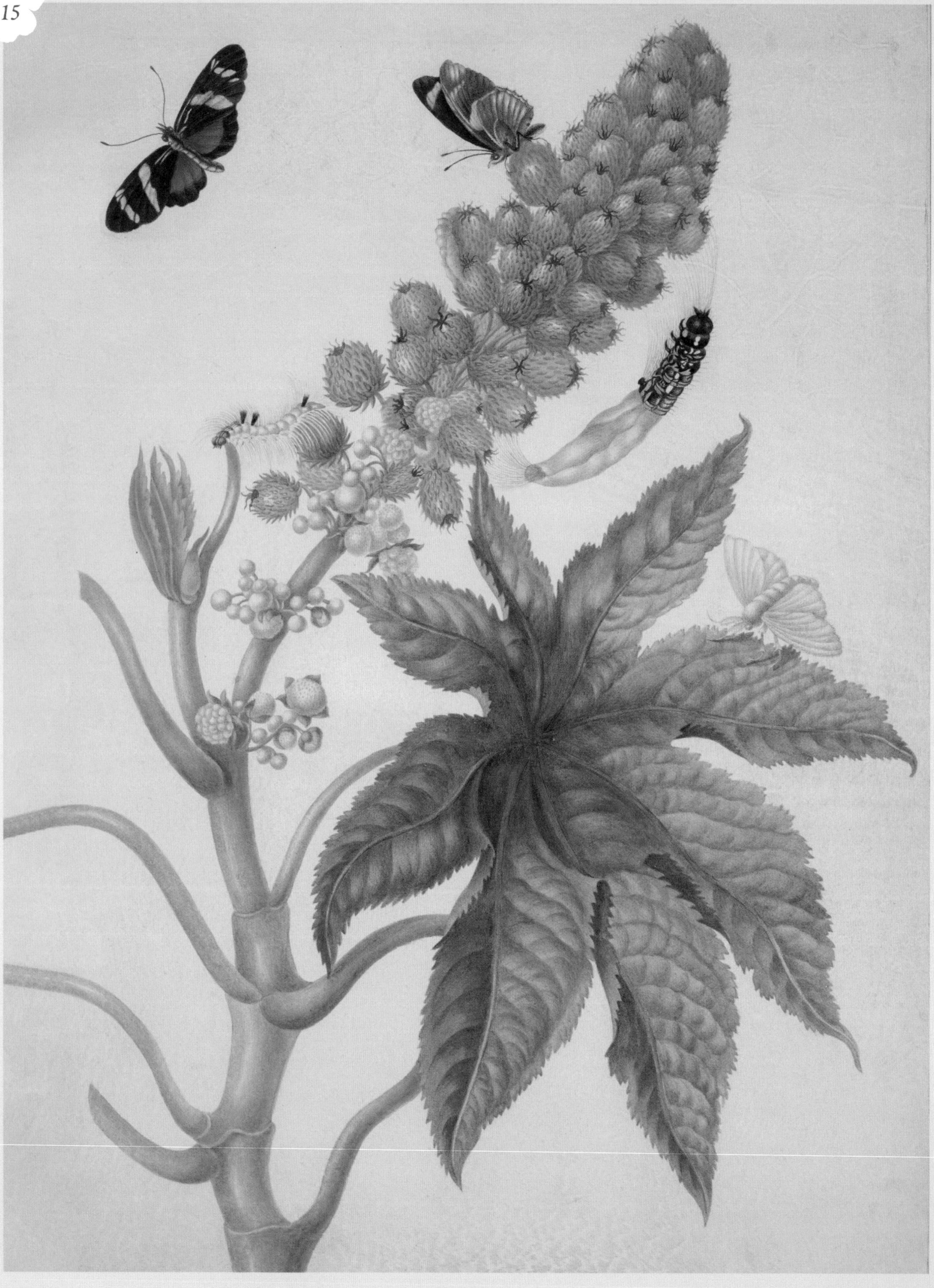

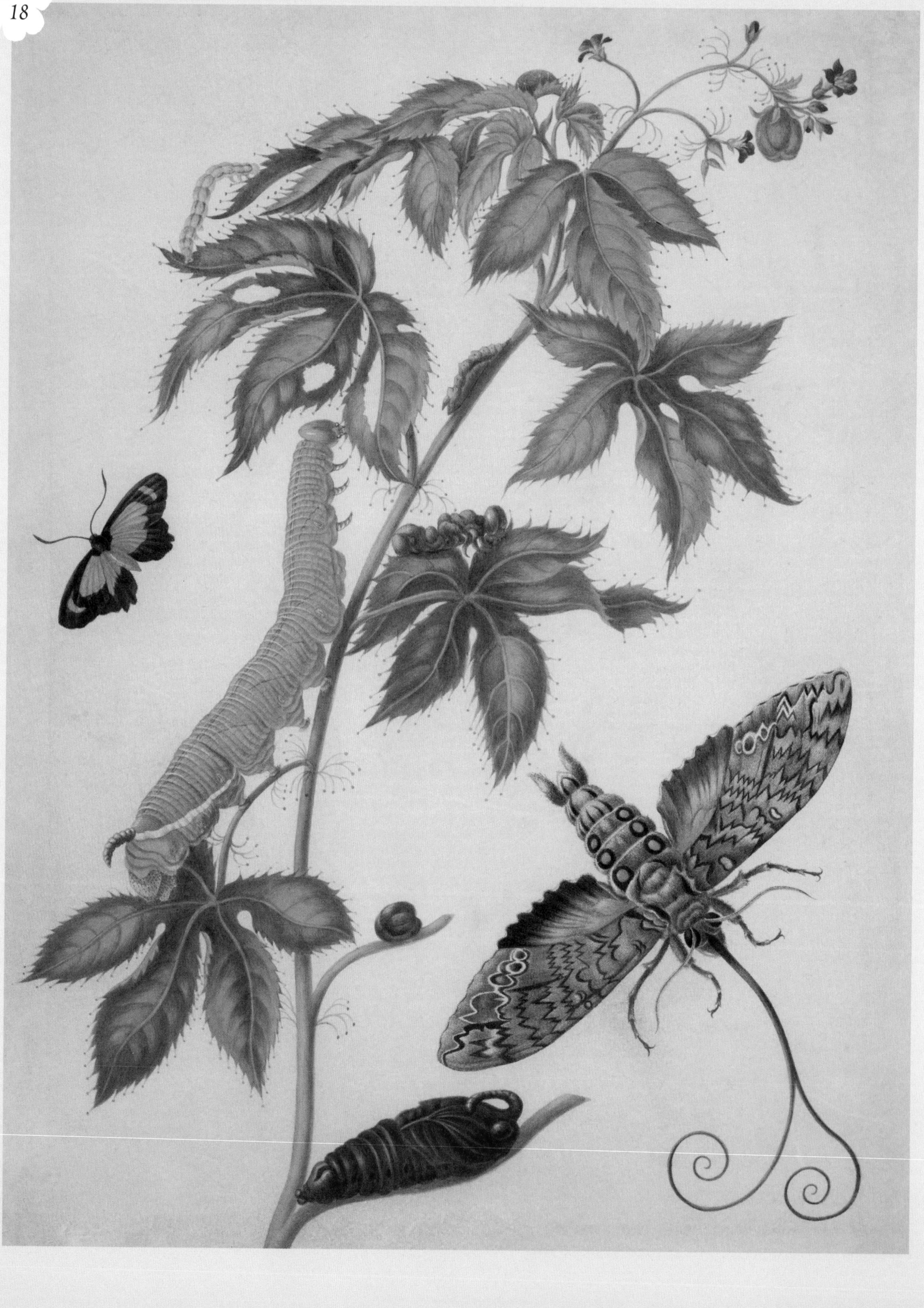

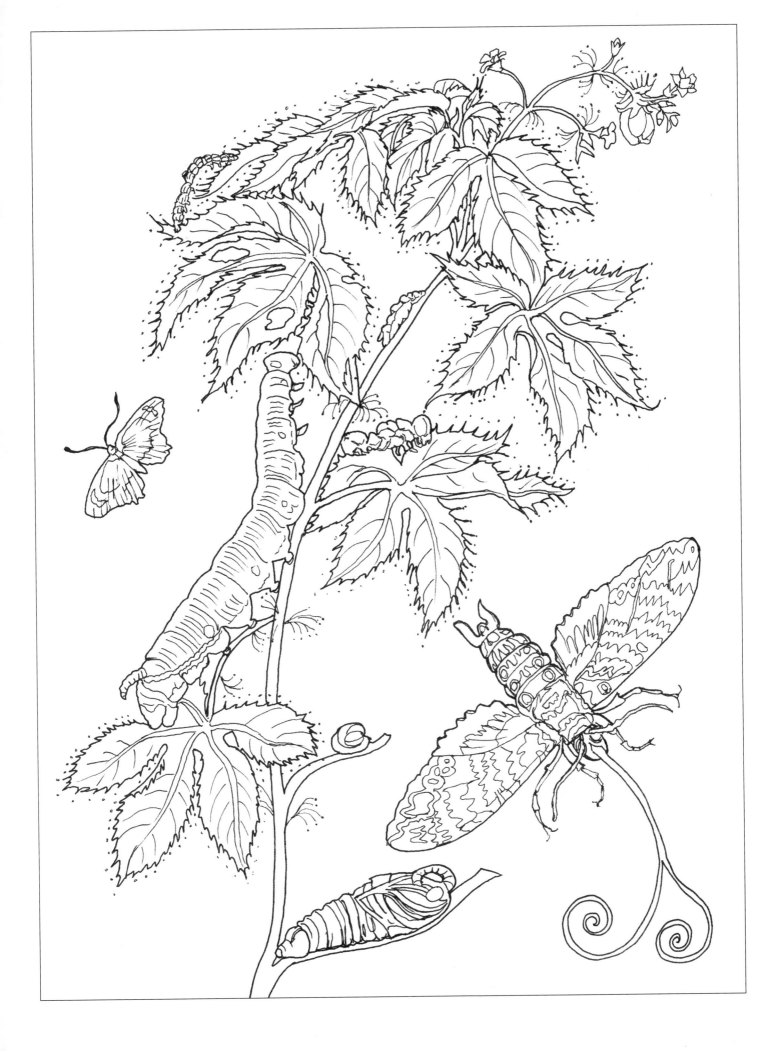

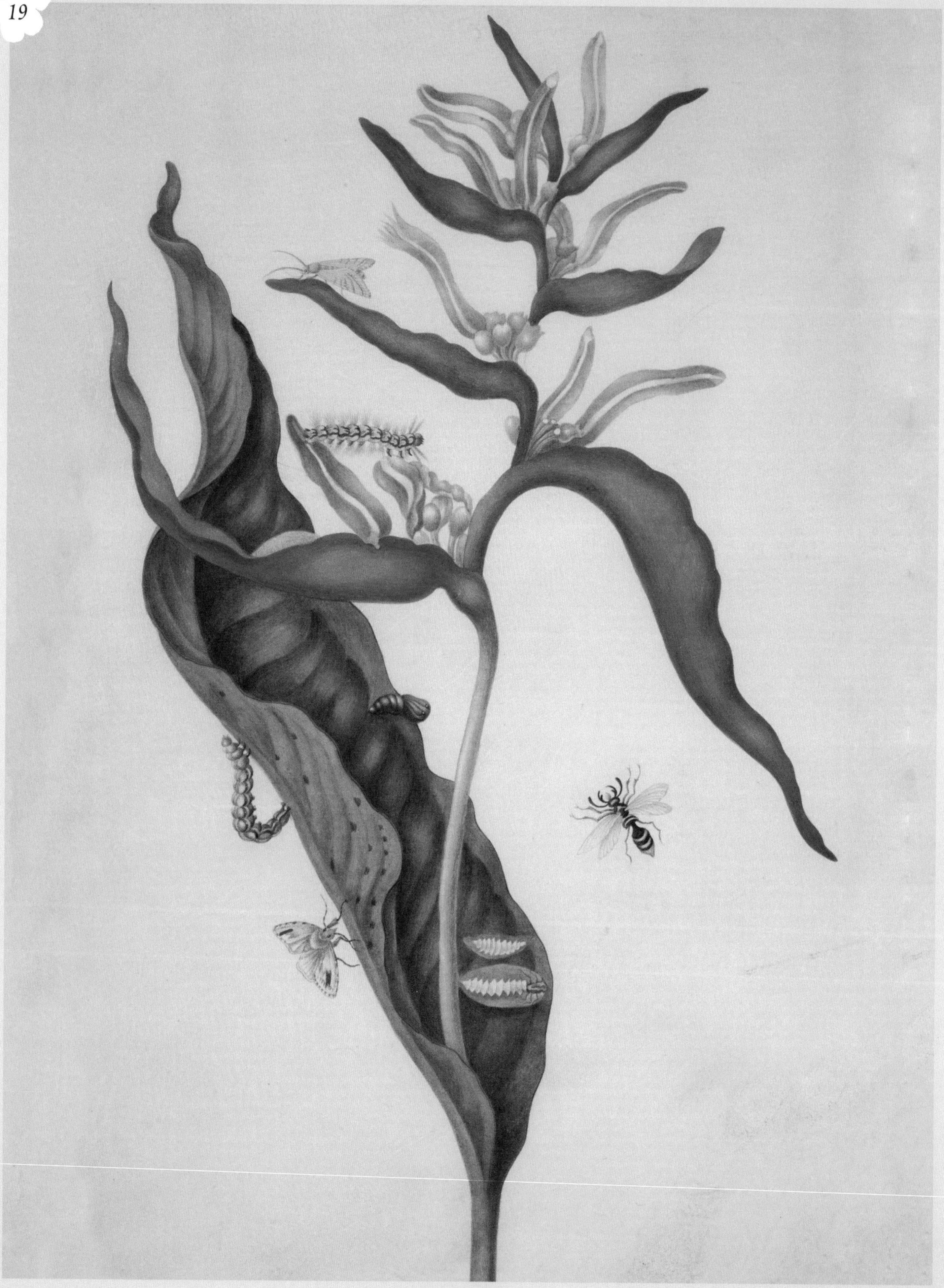

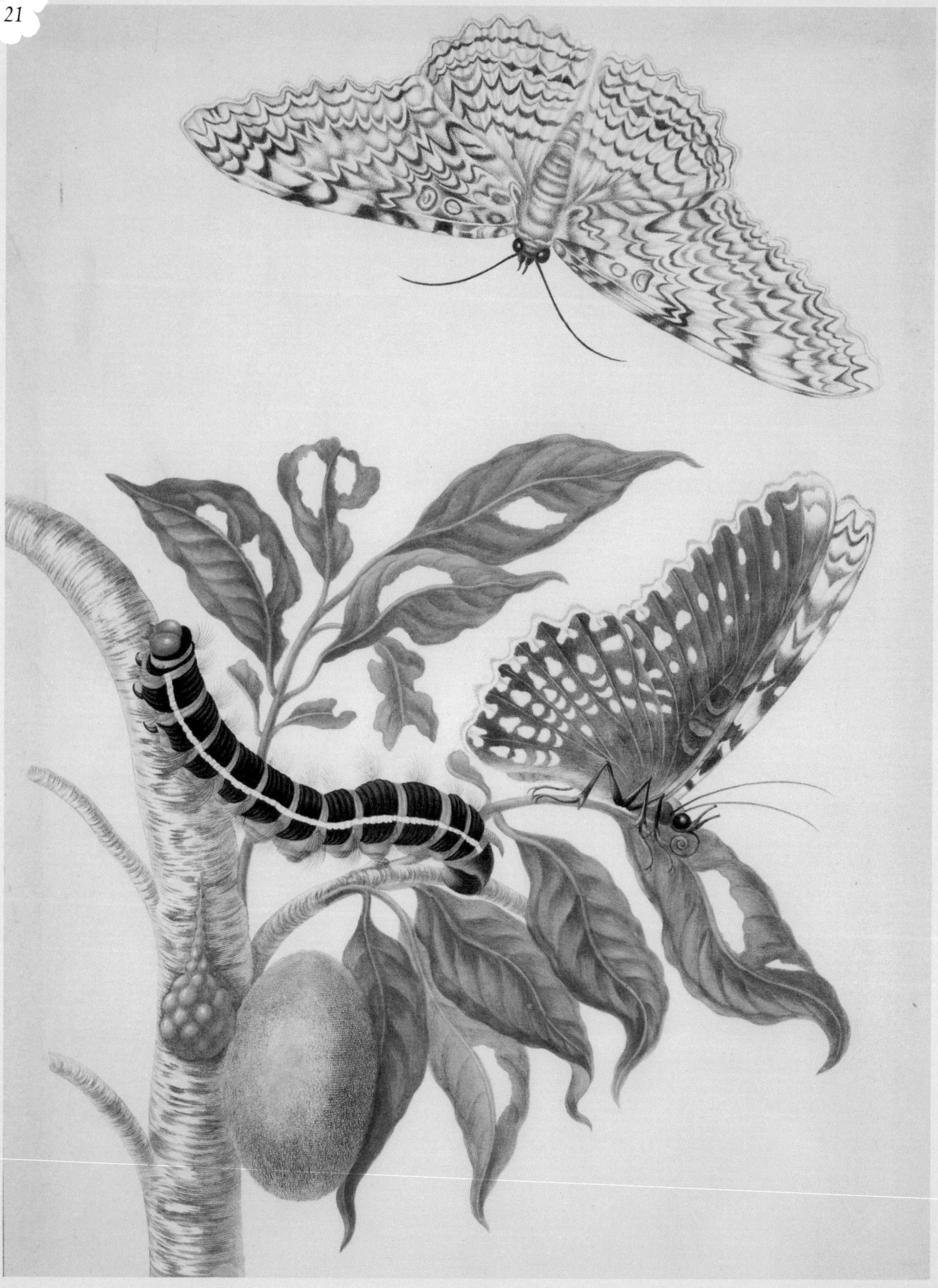

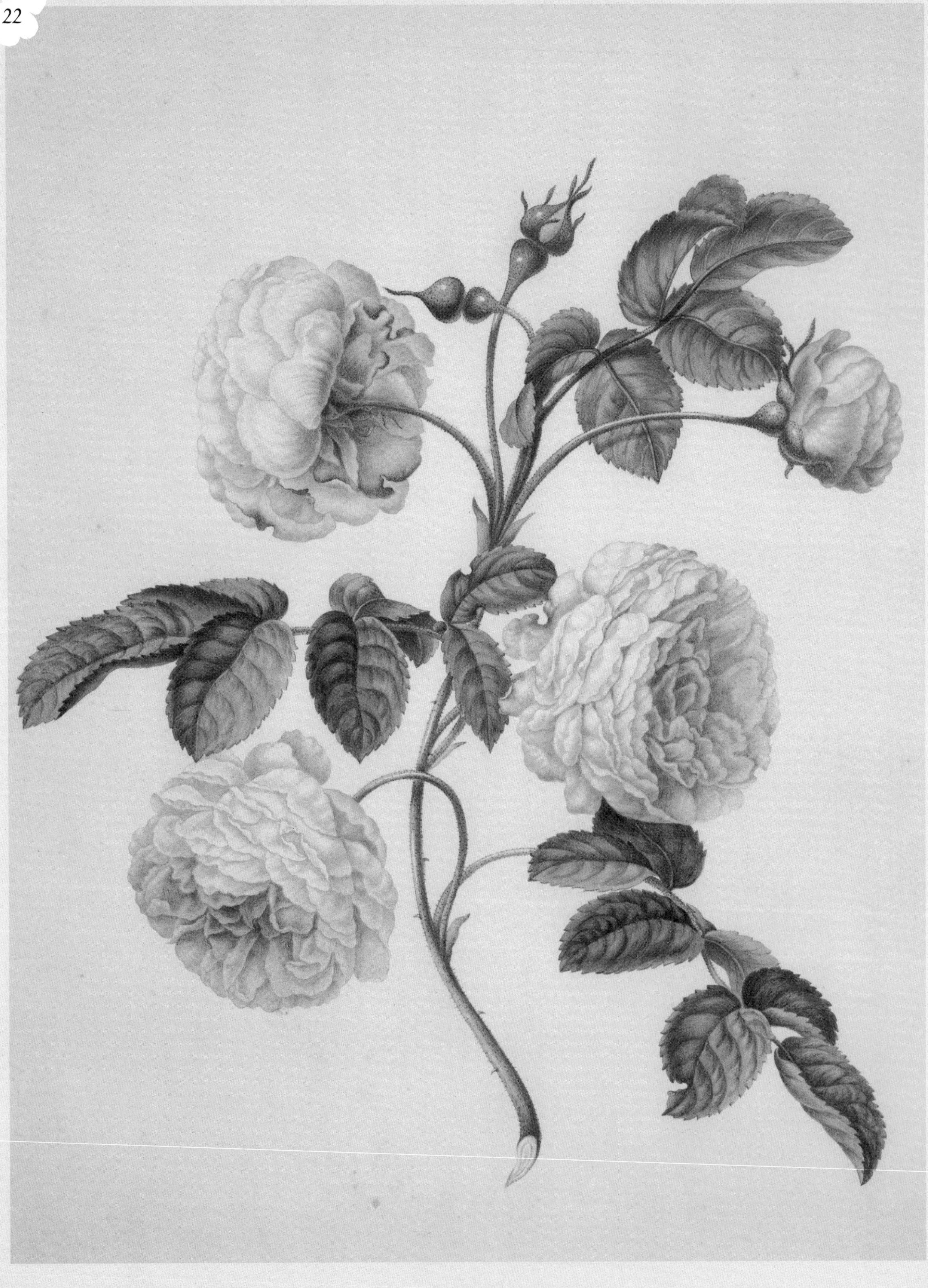

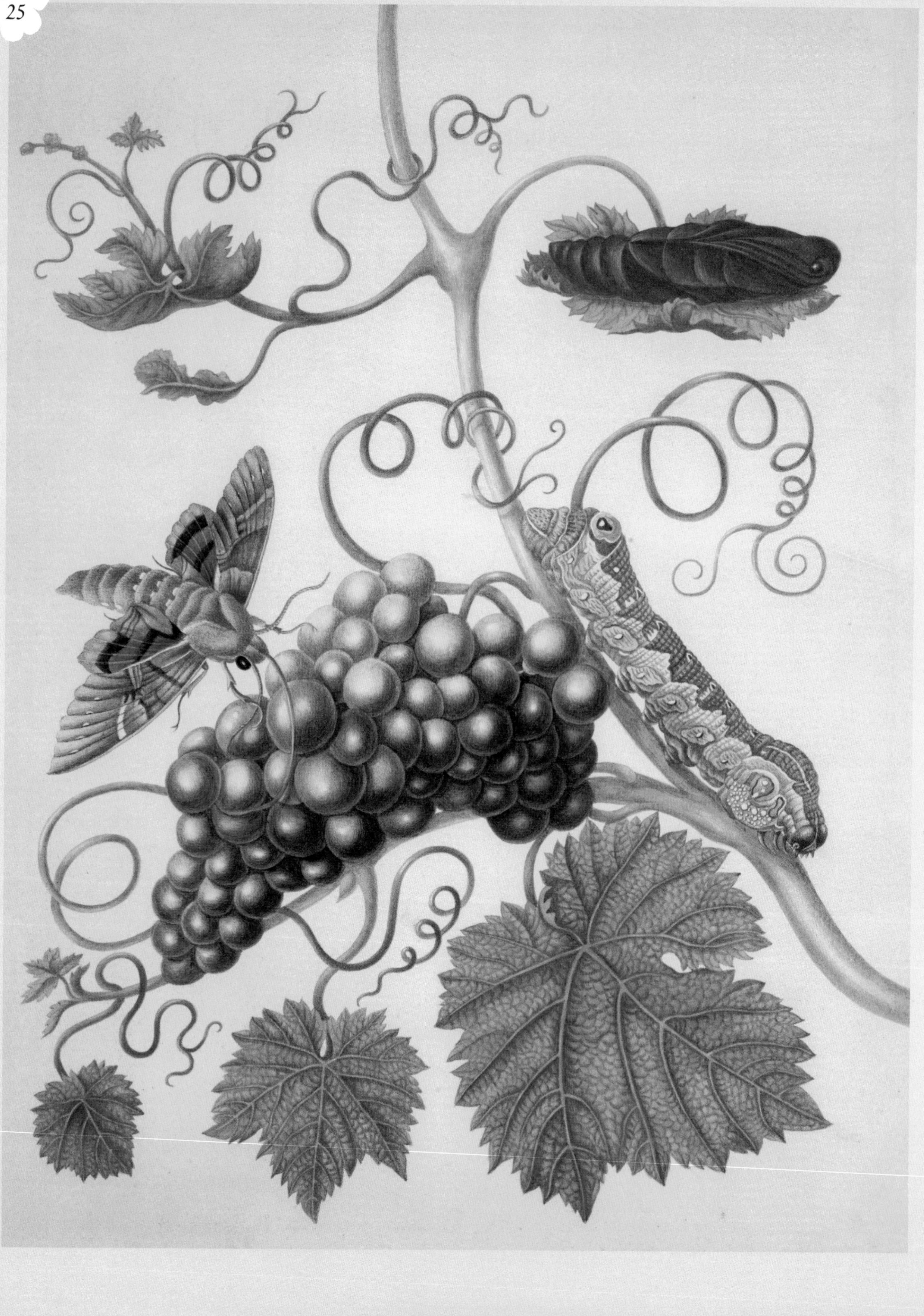

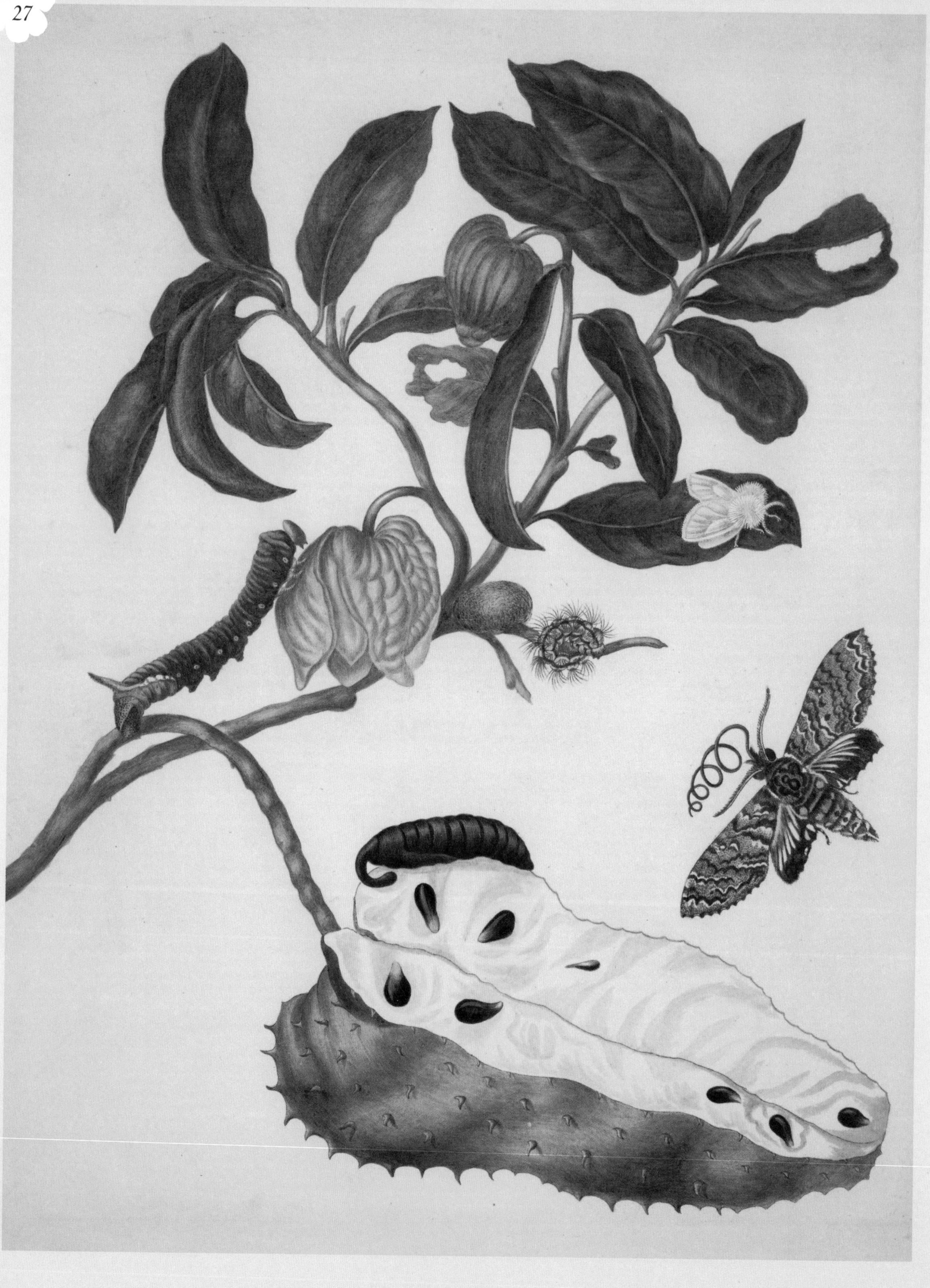

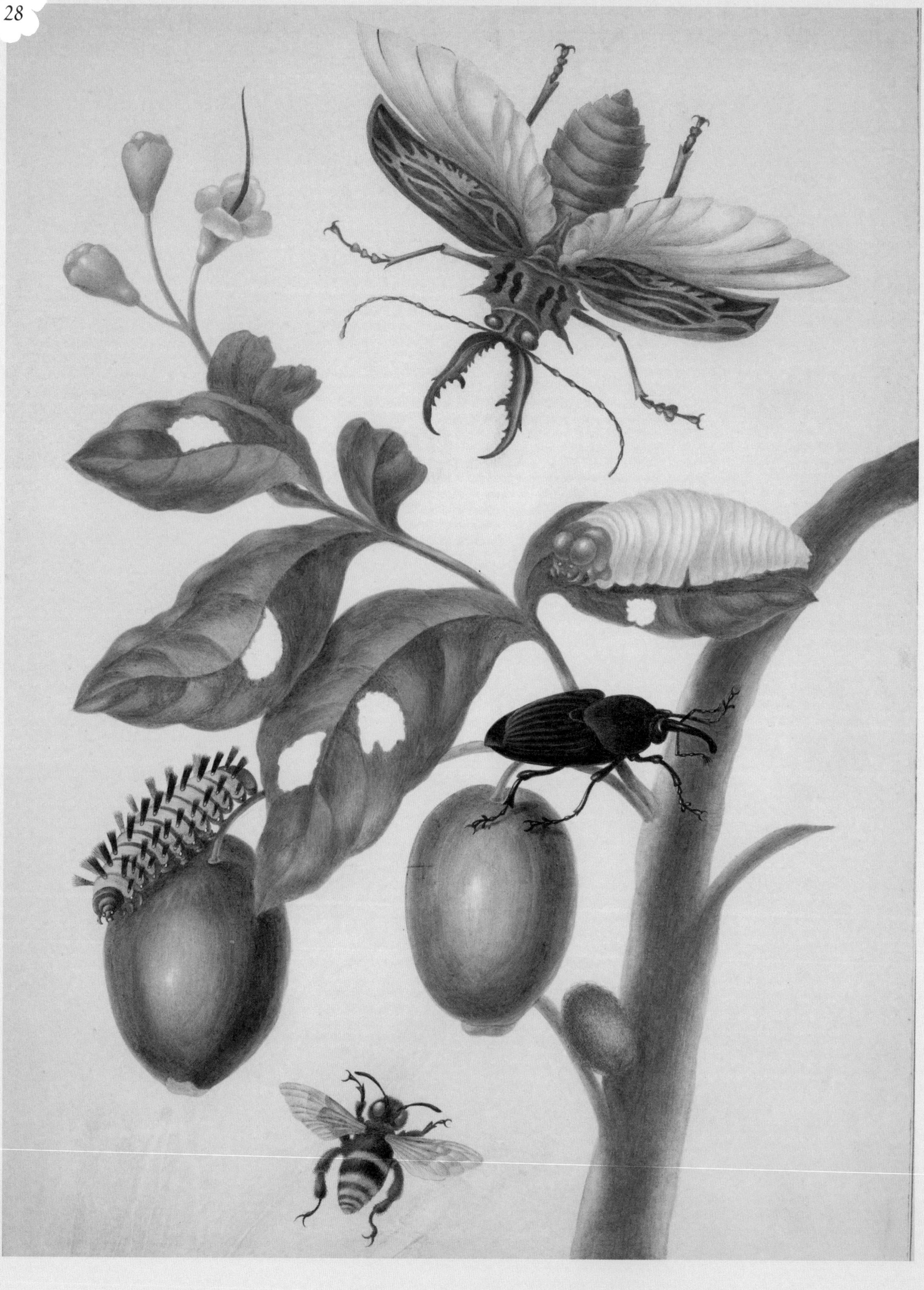

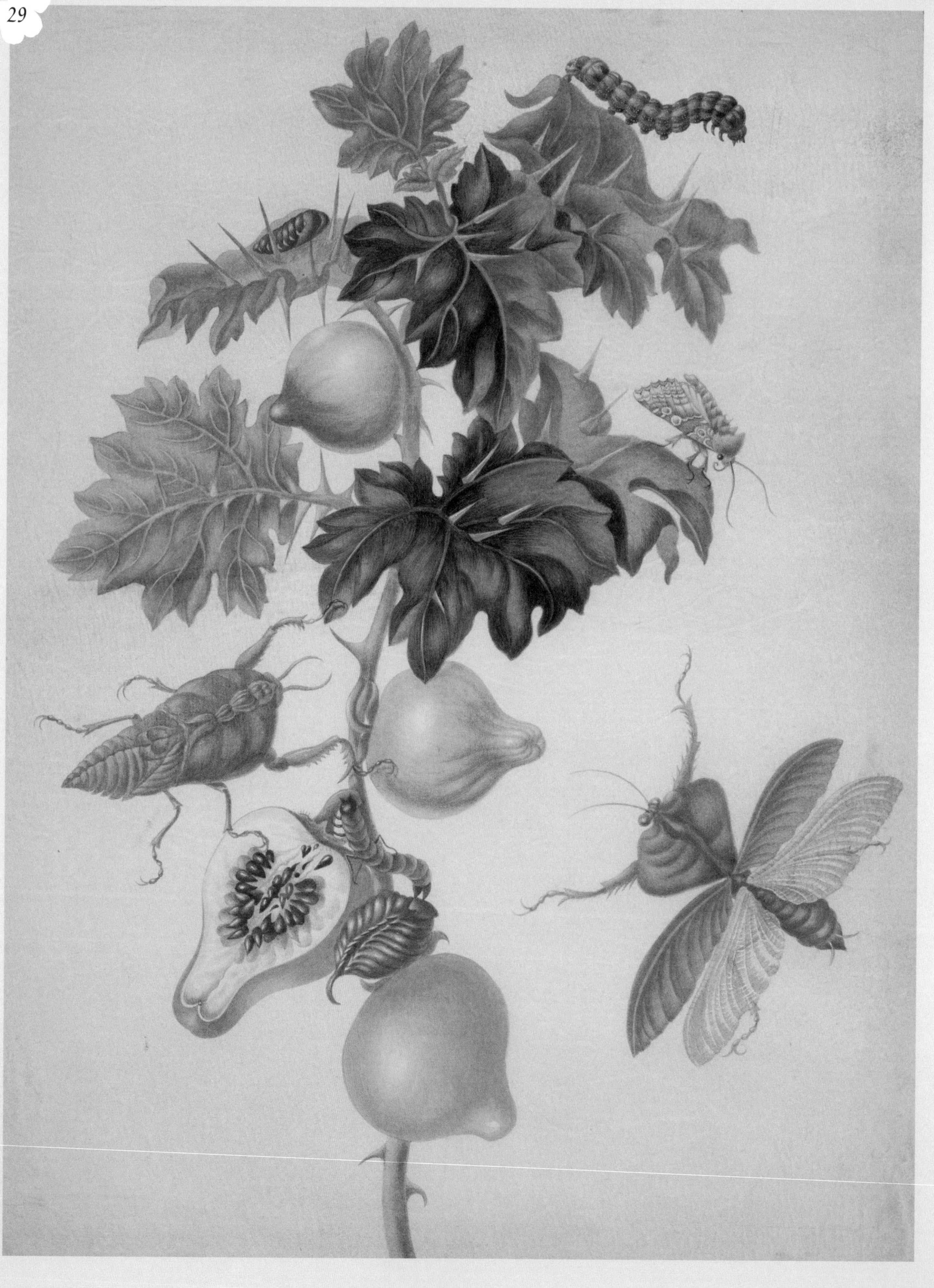

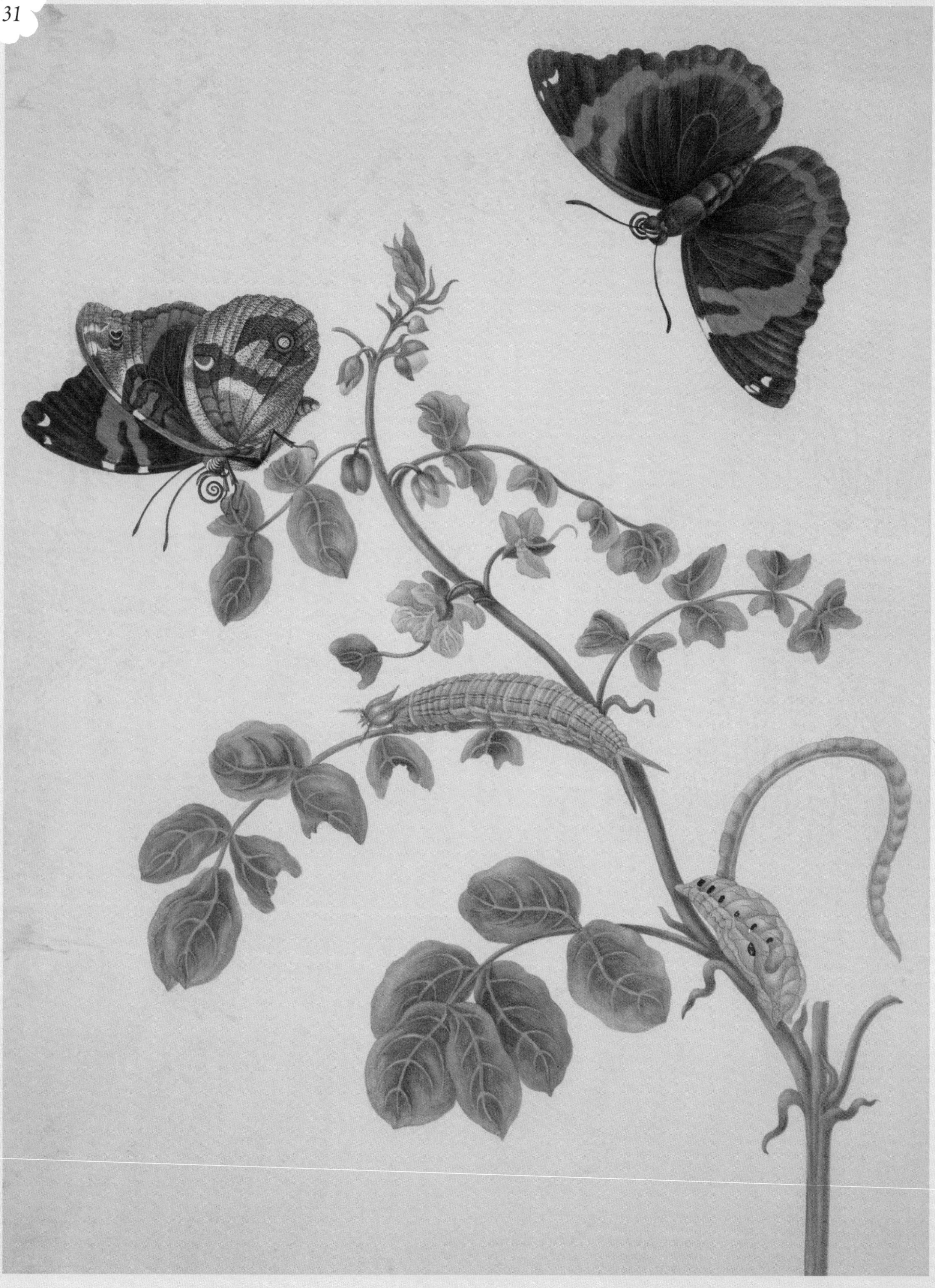

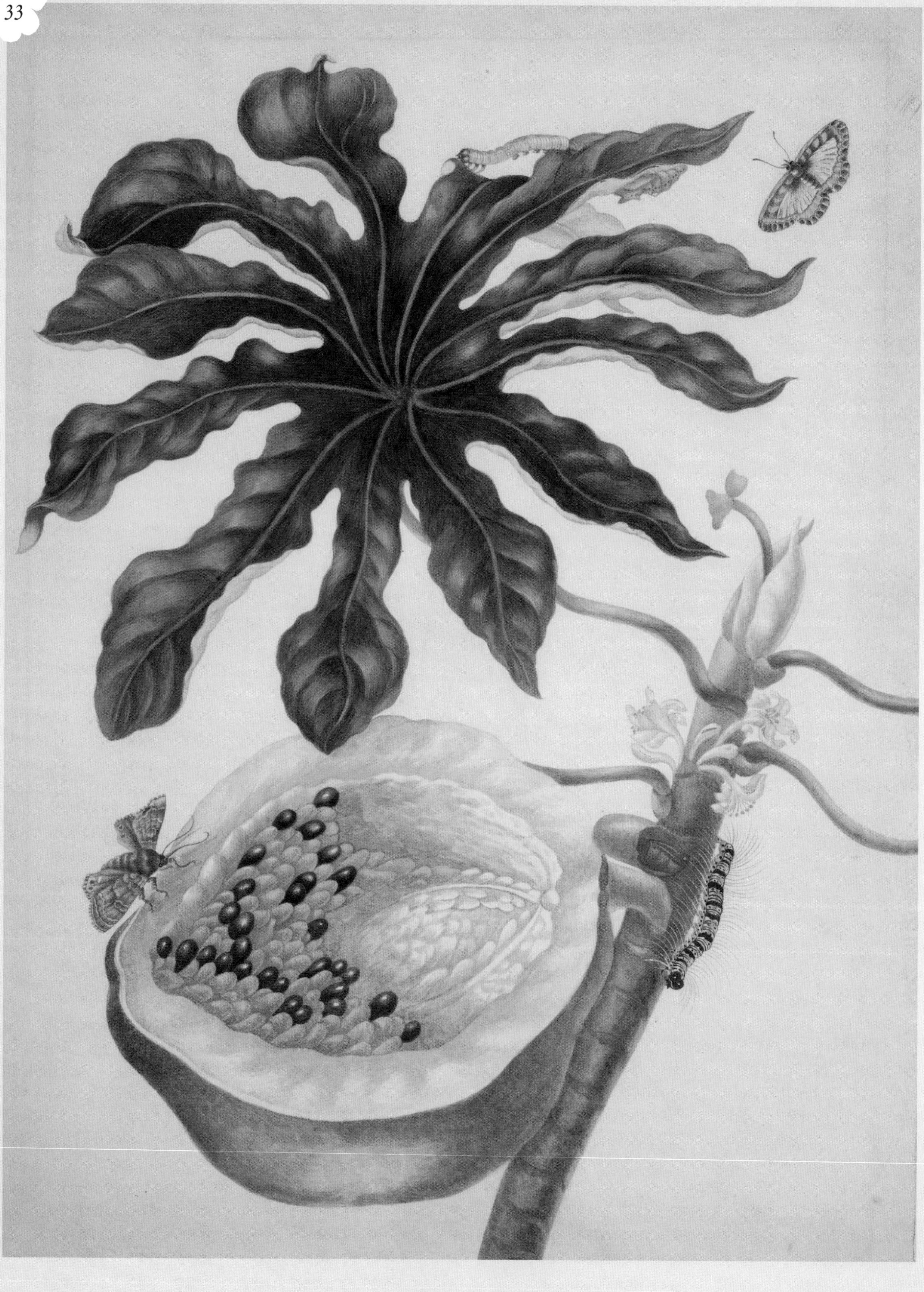

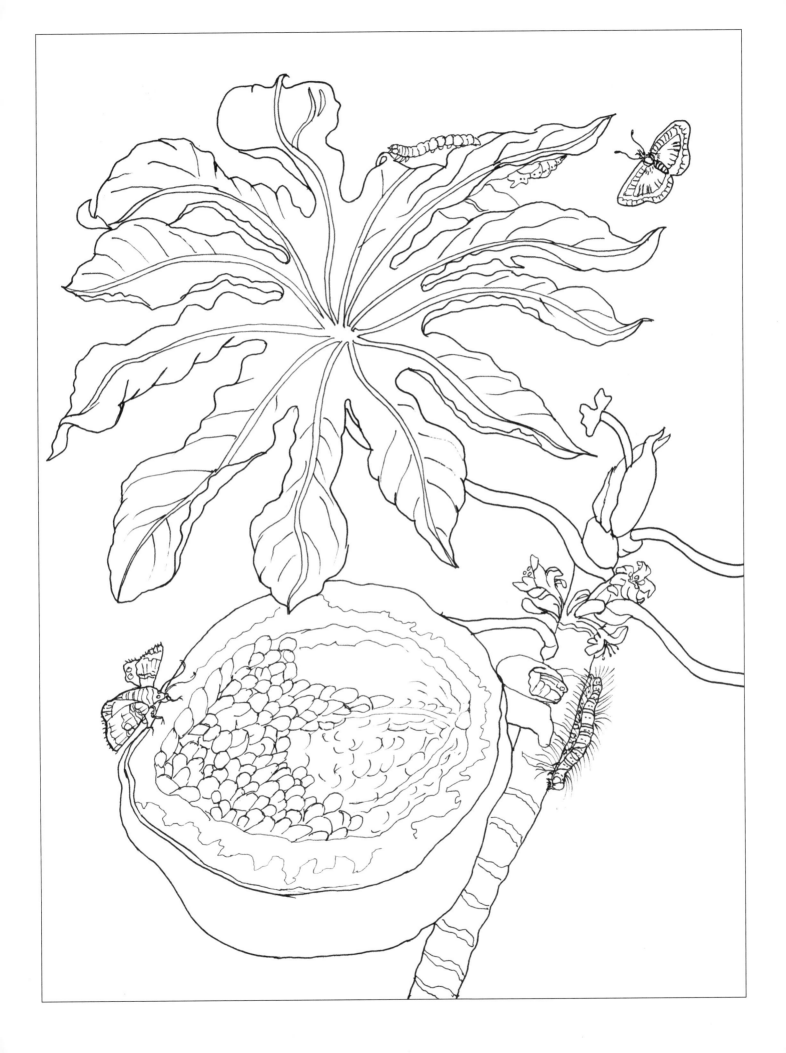

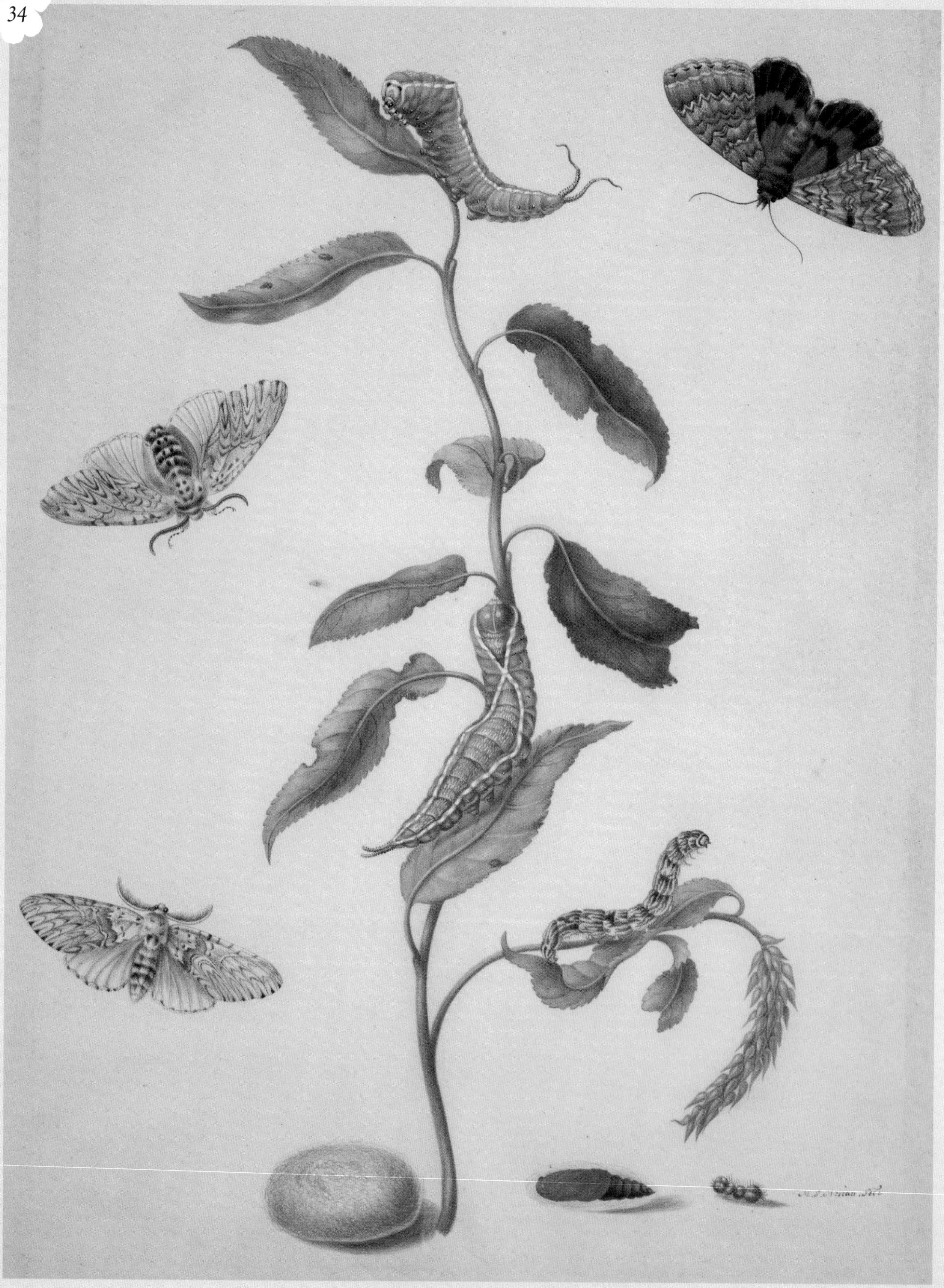

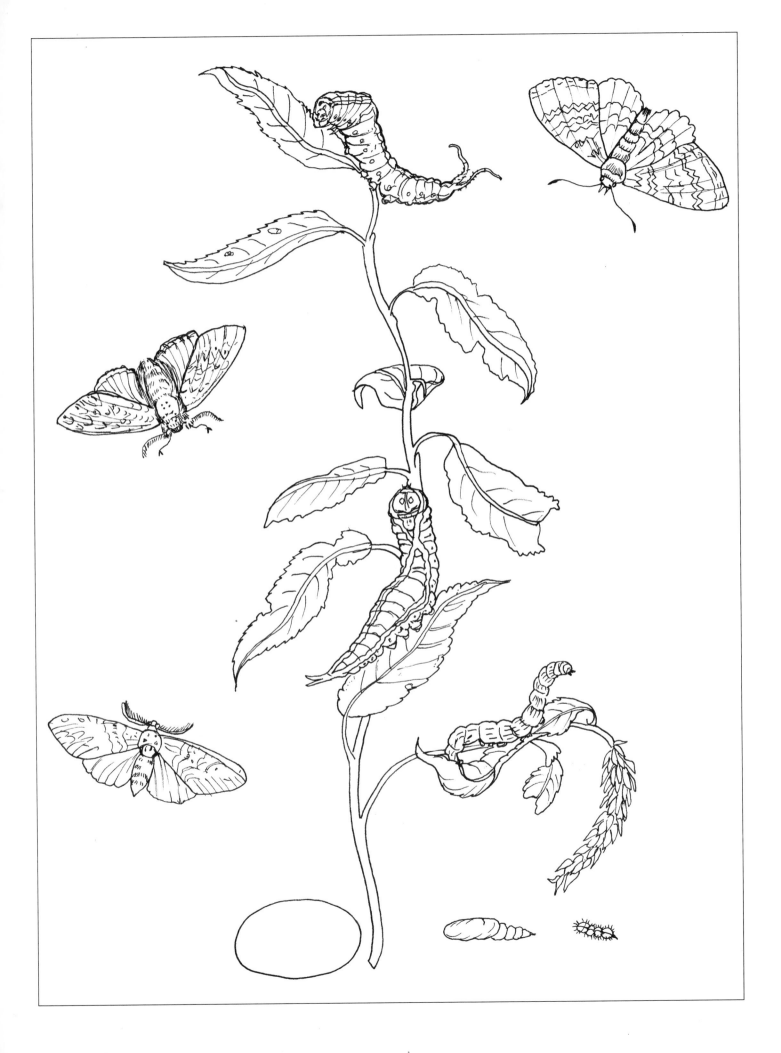

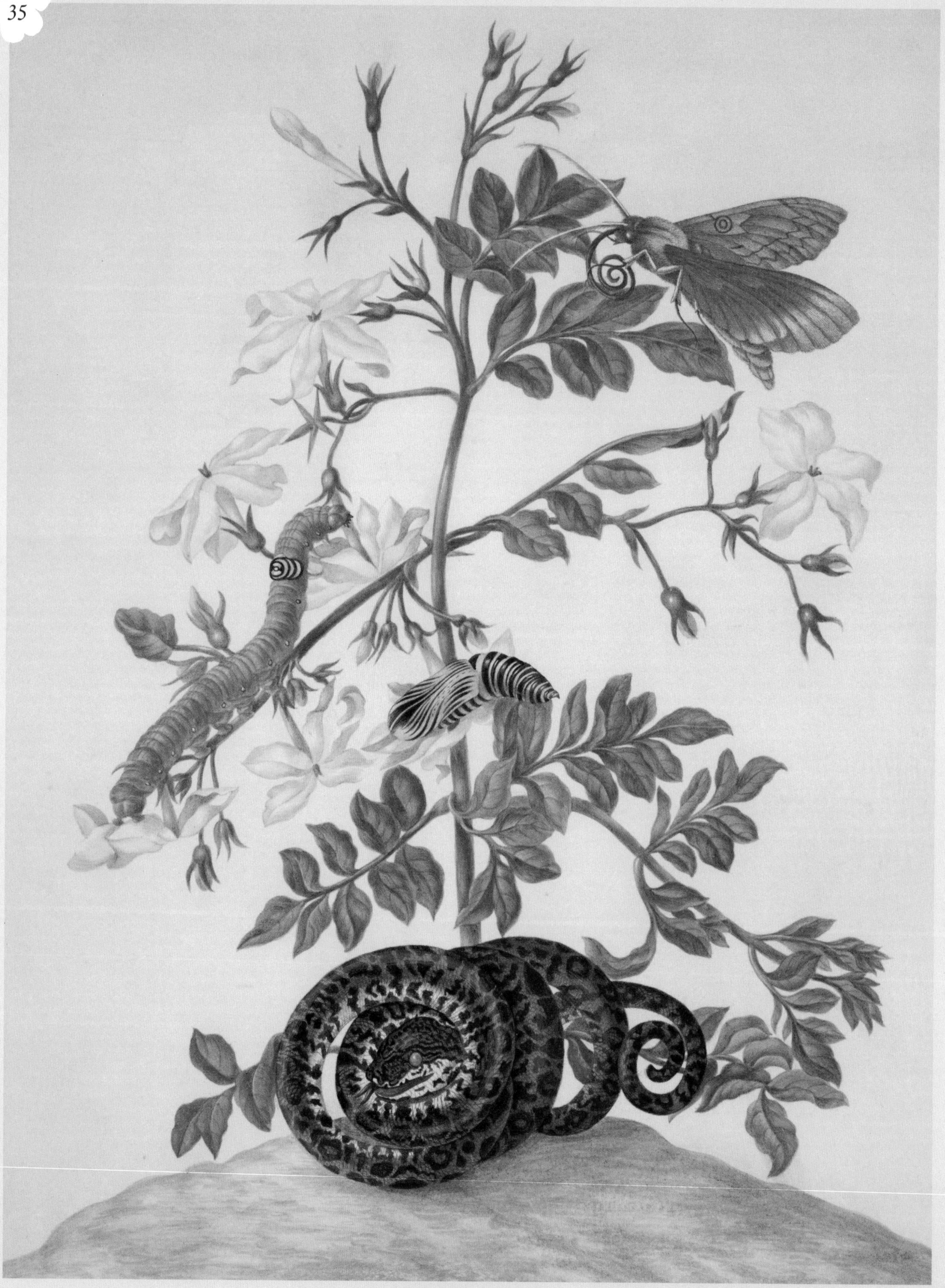

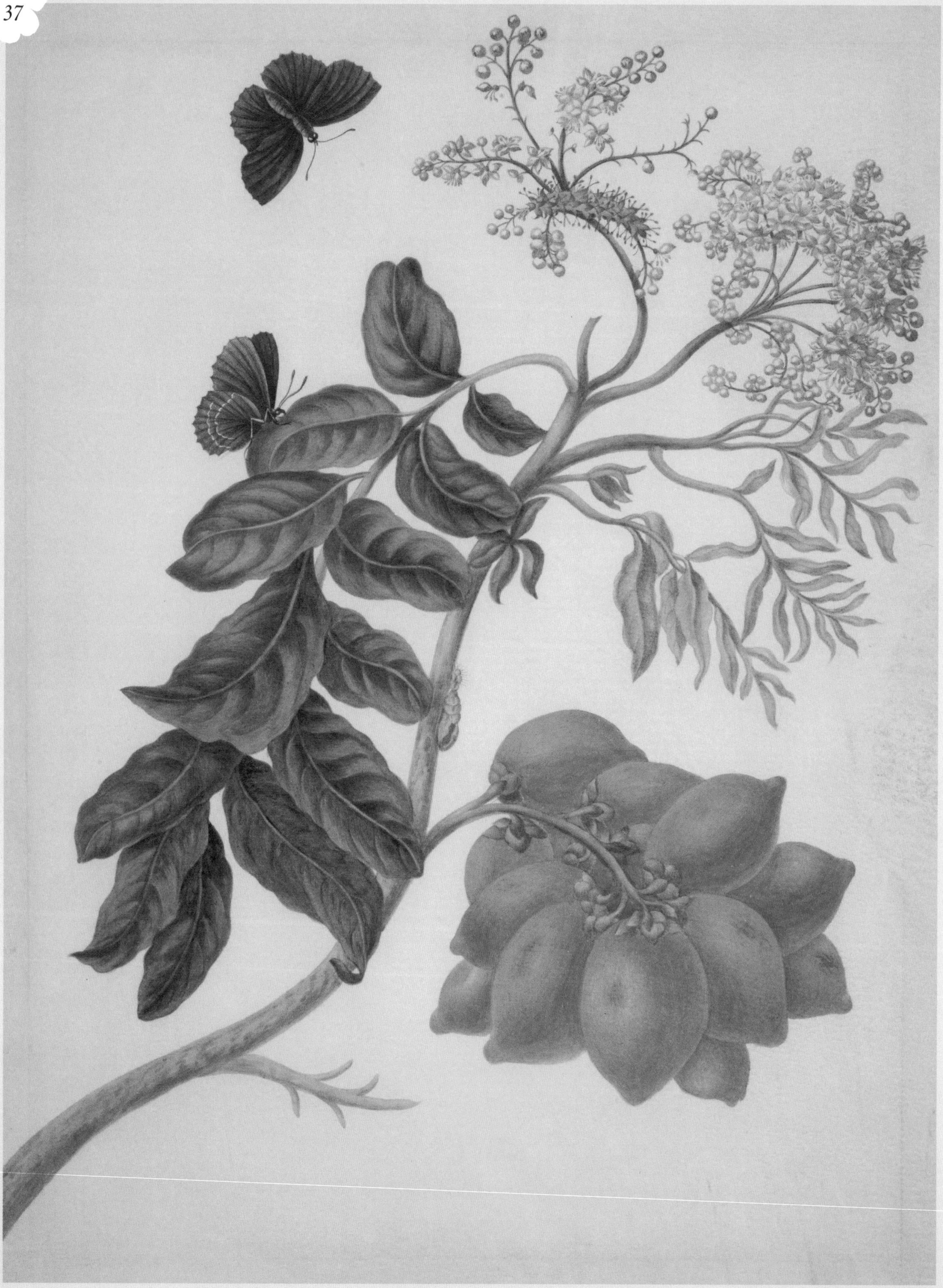

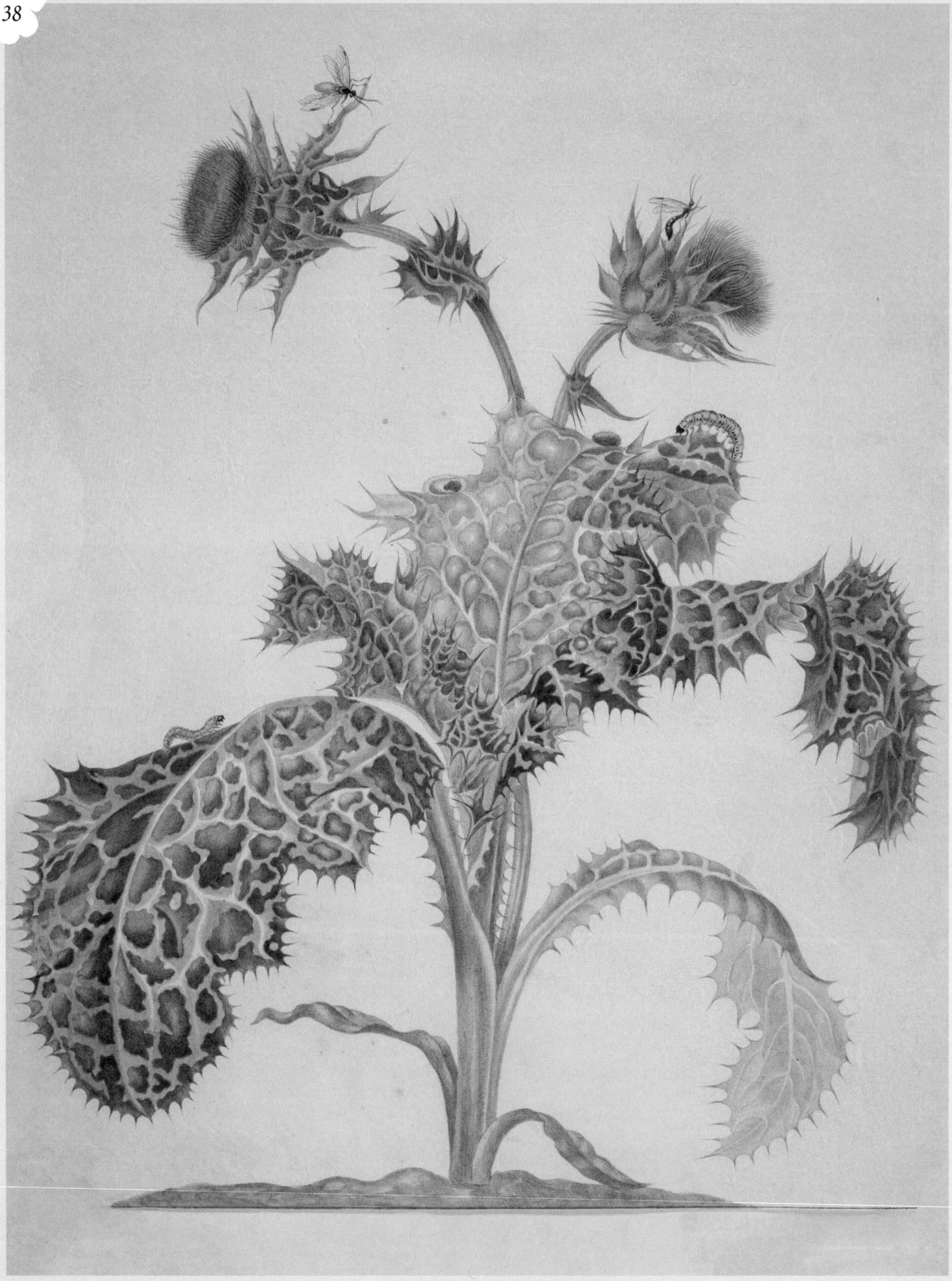

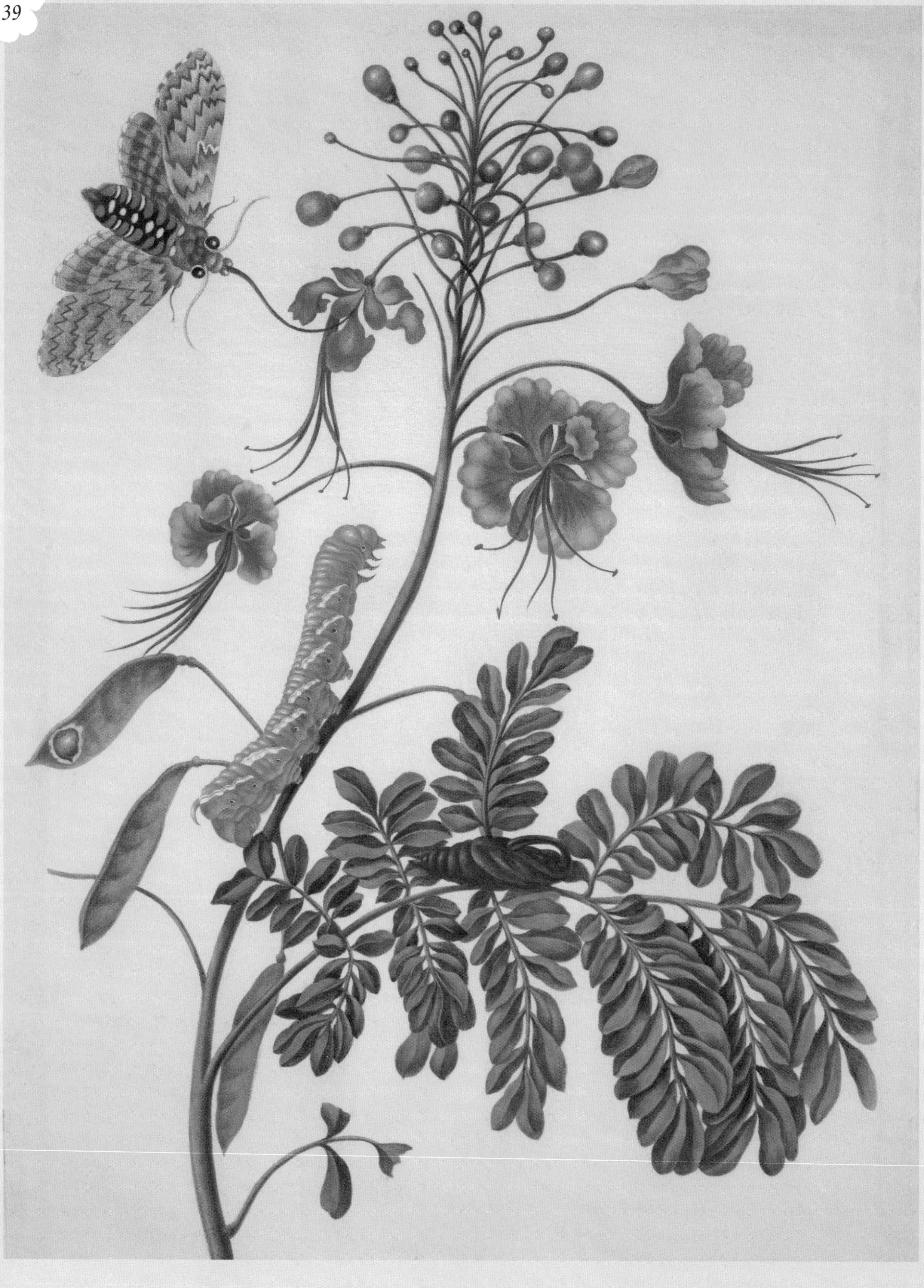

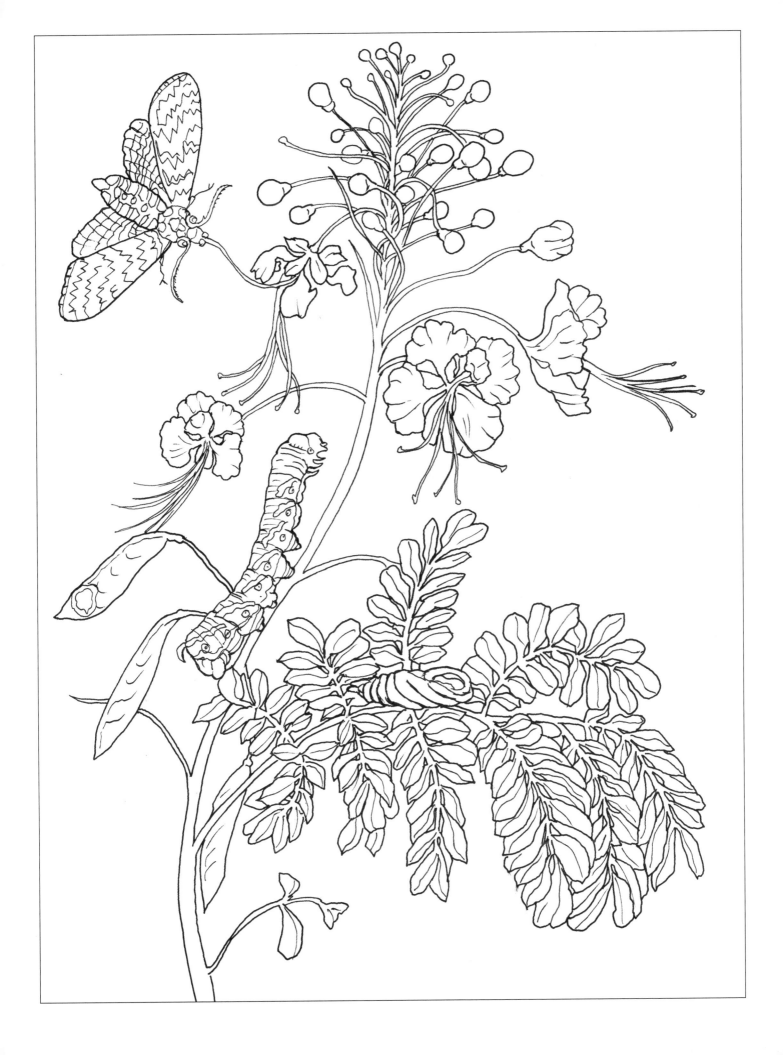

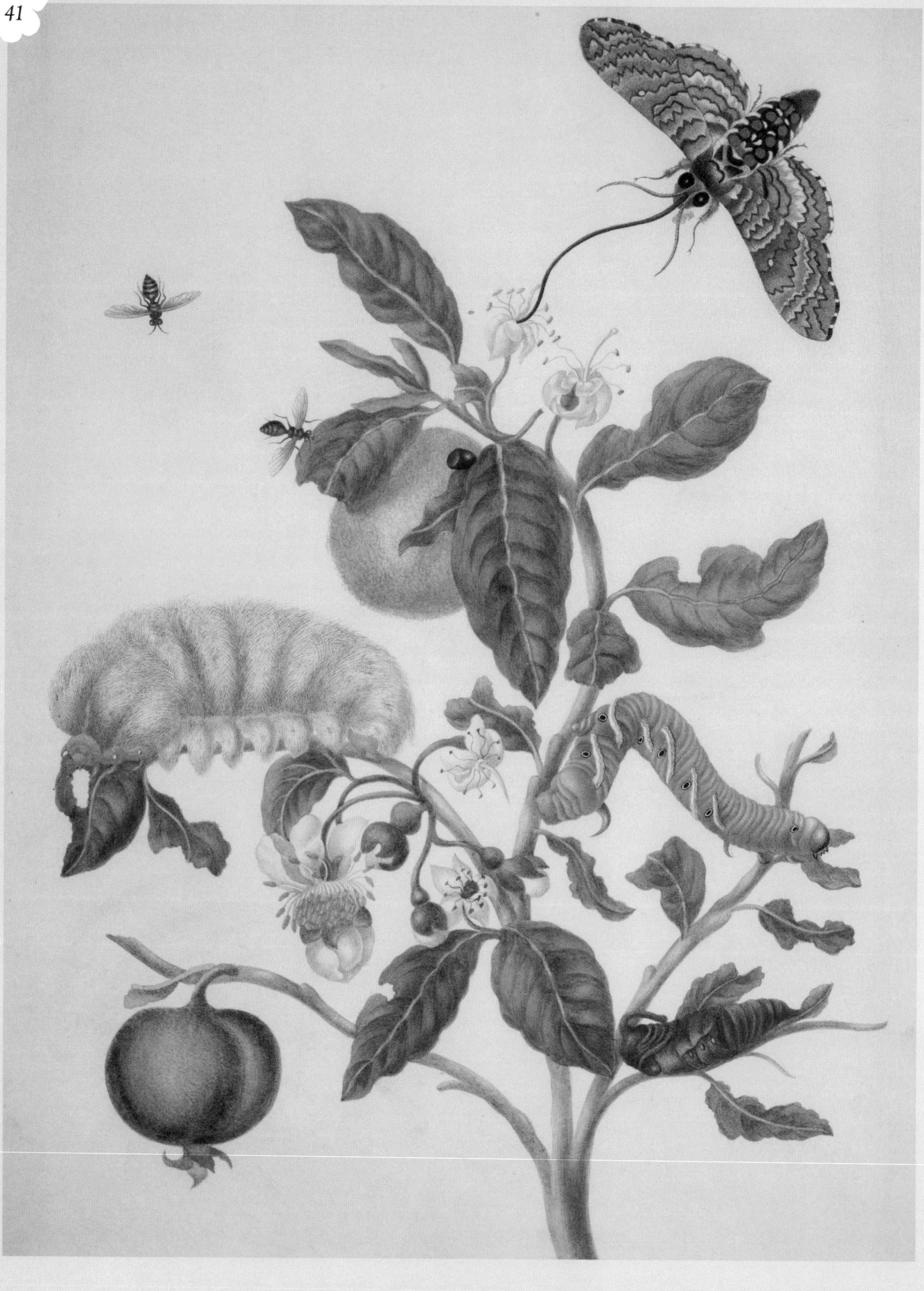

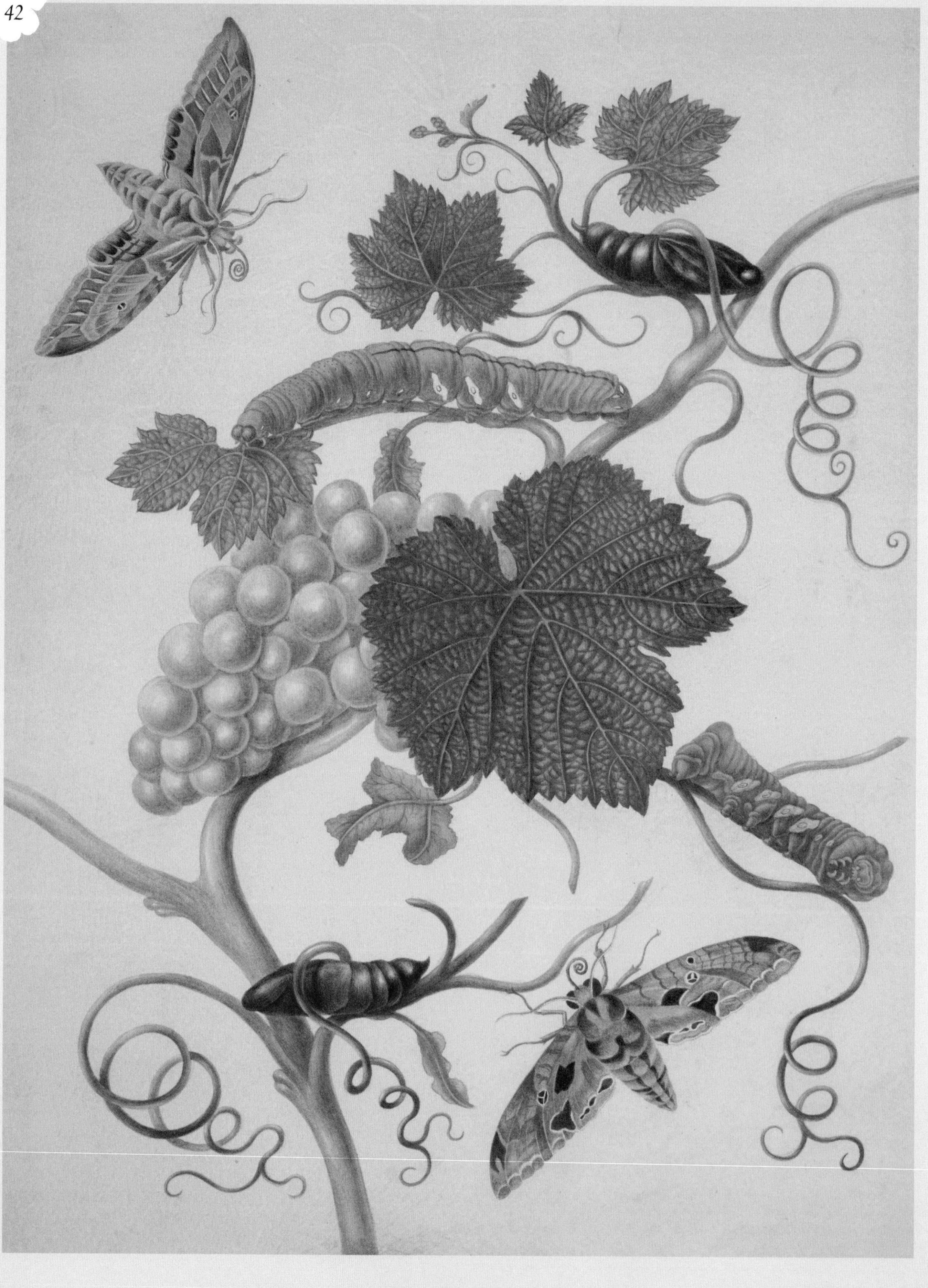

M. S. Merian. fec.

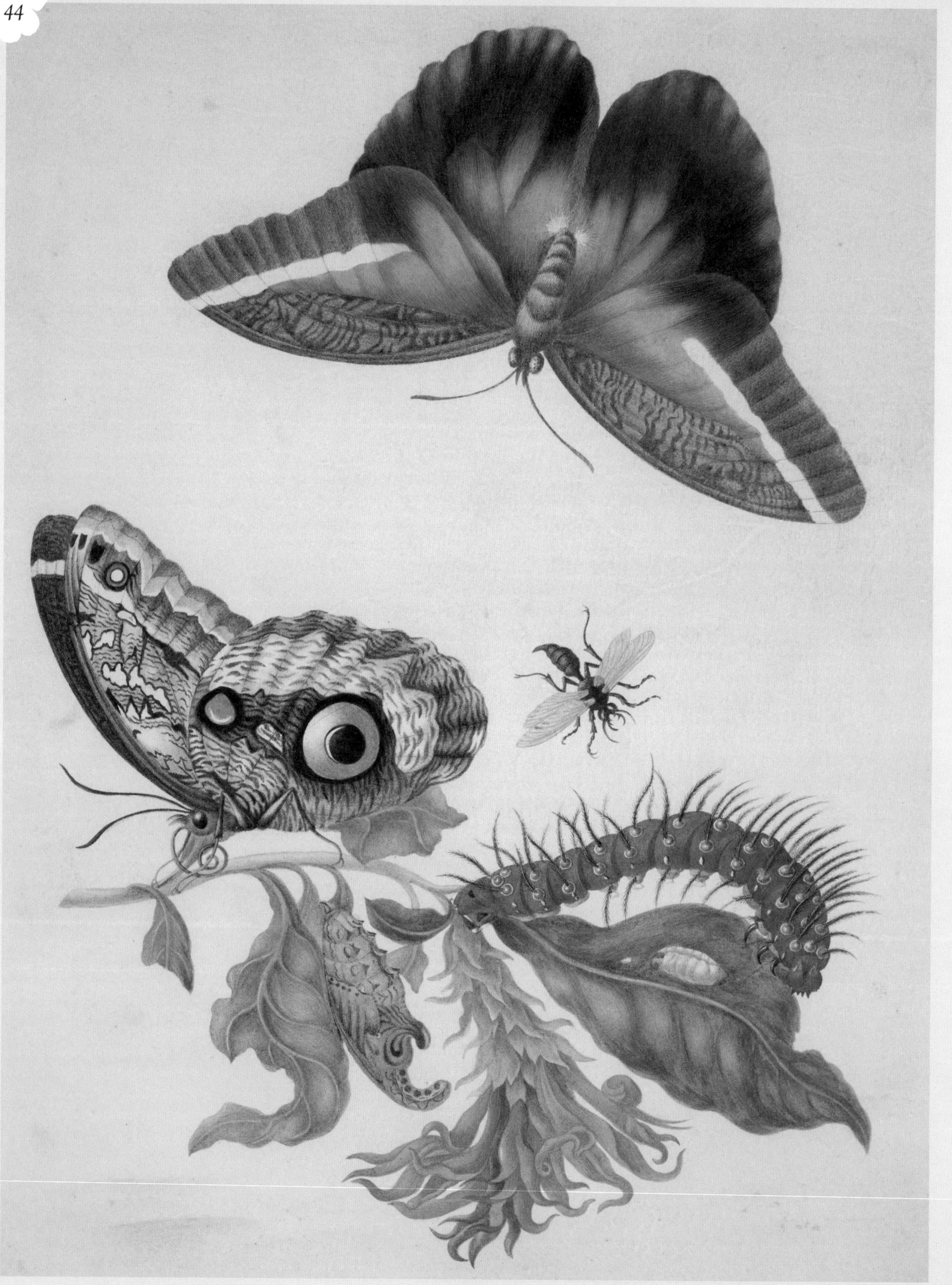